Unsent DMs

Unread. Unsent. Still True.

By Estelle Hartley

Unsent DMs

Unread. Unsent. Still True.

Copyright © 2025 Estelle Hartley

This is a work of creative nonfiction. While drawn from real emotional experiences, all messages are fictionalized or anonymized. Any resemblance to real people is purely coincidental.

For more work by Estelle Hartley, visit **farbellum.com**

Published by Farbellum Press
ISBN: [978-1-7641306-8-4] - Paperback

Cover design by Farbellum

First edition, 2025

Contents

Introduction 4

Beginnings 5

Hope 15

Love..23

Admiration 31

Becoming..39

Forgiveness..47

Guilt 55

Regret 62

Jealousy 70

Anger..78

Loneliness...86

Moments...94

Closure 102

Truths.. 109

Freedom... 117

Introduction

We write so many messages we never send.

Some were too honest. Some were too late.
Some we still type and delete, over and over.

This book is for those moments. The ones that
didn't make it into the thread, but never left us
either. Quiet things. Half-drafted thoughts.

Confessions that almost made it out.

Some of these were mine. Some will feel like
they were yours all along.

Some might feel like they were sent to you, even
if they never arrived.

You're not the only one who wrote it and
backspaced. You're not the only one who waited
for a reply that never came.

These are the unsent DMs. *Unread. Unsent. Still
true.*

Beginnings

The moment you smiled back, I knew everything would be different.

■■■

Yesterday ended. That's enough reason to begin again.

Beginnings

You'll never understand why I left.

You don't need to.

Because I do. And this is the start of me now.

■■

They didn't break us.

They won't.

Every day is a choice. And today, we begin again.

Beginnings

I didn't know it was the beginning.

That's how the best things start, isn't it?

■■■■■■■■■■■■■■■■■■■■■■■■■■■■■■■■■■■■■■

I was afraid of everything until that first night.

You didn't fix me. But you reminded me I
existed.

Beginnings

The first time you said my name like it mattered.
That's when it began.

■■

We didn't plan this.

And that's the only reason it felt real.

Beginnings

No one tells you the beginning might not look like joy.

Sometimes it looks like finally walking away.

■■

This time, I'm not proving anything.

This time, I'm just beginning.

Beginnings

I wasn't healed when I met you.

But I wanted to try being honest. That was new.

■■

We didn't even know what we were starting.

That's what made it beautiful. And dangerous.

Beginnings

You made space without knowing.

That was the first time I breathed differently.

■■ ■■

This isn't a comeback.

It's a beginning. And it's mine.

Beginnings

We said hi at the same time.

I think about that more than I should.

■■

The way your eyes softened.

I think that was the moment I started unfolding.

Beginnings

There wasn't a moment, really. Just a slow opening. And that was enough.

■ ■

There was a version of me before you.

I didn't know how much I'd miss her.

I'm still trying to find my way back.

Beginnings

I said it didn't matter.

But I smiled all the way home.

∎∎∎

You didn't say much.

But I breathed differently around you.

Hope

I still believe there's a version of you that meant it.

■■■■■■■■■■■■■■■■■■■■■■■■■■■■■■■■■■■■■■■ ■■

Some part of me thinks you'll reach out the second I stop waiting.

Hope

I don't know if we'll ever talk again.

But I keep practicing what I'd say if we did.

■■

I hope one day you understand why I pulled away.

It wasn't because I stopped caring.

Hope

Maybe you're not gone.

Maybe you're just getting ready to come back different.

■■

I still check your name in the group thread.

Just in case you come back

.

Hope

I reread our last message like it's a door I haven't given up on.

■■

If this isn't the end, maybe it's just a long pause.

Hope

I hope the version of me you remember isn't just the worst one.

∎∎∎∎∎∎∎∎∎∎∎∎∎∎∎∎∎∎∎∎∎∎∎∎∎∎∎∎∎∎∎∎∎∎∎∎∎∎

I don't need you to come back.

I just need to believe it's possible.

Hope

Sometimes hope is quiet.

Like checking your profile and not refreshing.

■■■

I still imagine you reading this.

That has to mean something.

Hope

You said you were proud of me once.

I hope that would still be true.

■■■

This message is for the future

The one where we understand each other.

Hope

If we meet again, I hope we recognize what we couldn't back then.

■■

I kept the light on a little longer tonight.

Just in case you were on your way.

Love

You made me laugh in the middle of a sentence I was crying through.

That was love too

■■

For a while, we forgot the world.

And that's what I keep

.

Love

It wasn't the way you looked at me.

It was the way I looked at you when you weren't.

■■■■■■■■■■■■■■■■■■■■■■■■■■■■■■■■■■■■■ ■■

I never told you.

Not because I didn't feel it.

But because I knew you didn't.

Love

I loved you in a quiet way.

That's probably why you never noticed.

■ ■

You didn't have to love me back.

But you didn't have to pretend, either.

Love

I thought if I loved you well enough,

you'd want to stay.

You taught me how to love deeply.

And then you taught me what it costs.

Love

Some of me stayed with you.

But most of me walked away whispering, "please notice."

■■■■■■■■■■■■■■■■■■■■■■■■■■■■■■■■■■■■■ ■■

You didn't ruin me.

You just made everything after feel smaller.

Love

It wasn't forever.

But it was enough to believe love was still possible.

■■■

Whatever it was, it made me softer.

And that has to count for something.

Love

There was a moment today — sunlight through dust, silence in traffic; and I loved being alive so quietly it hurt.

■■

I walked without knowing where.

Every step felt like remembering I still had a body.

Love

I forgive the version of me that only knew how to survive. She did her best with no instructions. I still love her.

■■■

It was just a cup of coffee, but I kept looking at it like it was the sunrise.

Admiration

You made me want to try again.

Not at life.

At being kind.

∎∎∎∎∎∎∎∎∎∎∎∎∎∎∎∎∎∎∎∎∎∎∎∎∎∎∎∎∎∎∎∎∎∎∎∎∎

You probably don't even remember what you said.

But I folded it up like a note and carried it with me for years.

Admiration

I know you don't know me.

But you made me feel like I could know myself.

■■

I watched the way you moved through the
world.

And without knowing, I started walking
straighter.

Admiration

It wasn't a big moment.

Just the way you looked up and listened.

But it made me feel worth listening to.

■■■

You said something once on a podcast — just a sentence.

I still hear it when I need to feel brave.

Admiration

You made me feel like I wasn't weird for caring this much.

That meant everything at the time.

■■■

You never noticed how many people paused when you spoke.

That's how I knew it wasn't performance.

Admiration

You'll never read this.

But your posts got me through nights when no
one else even knew I was breaking.

■■■

You didn't tell me what to do.

You just did it well enough that I wanted to
follow.

Admiration

You didn't teach me how to be loud.

You taught me how to be clear.

■■

You gave me permission to love the parts of
myself I used to hide.

Admiration

You were just being you.

But I was taking notes the whole time.

■■■■■■■■■■■■■■■■■■■■■■■■■■■■■■■■■■■■■■

I'm better because you existed.

Even if you never knew I did.

Admiration

You lived through things I only read about.

And still found time to smile at strangers.

That's the kind of strength I hope I carry
forward.

■■■

Dad, you were tired in ways I didn't understand.

But you still answered the door when I knocked.

That was love. Even if neither of us said it.

Becoming

I'm not who I was when this started.

And thank god for that.

■■

Some days I feel like a blank page. Other days, a whole chapter. Both are still becoming a book.

Becoming

I used to break myself to be small enough for other people.

Now I build space for the version of me that takes up room.

■■■

You wouldn't recognize me now.

And I think that's the best part.

Becoming

This isn't a comeback.

No Parade. No Balloons.

Just a quiet arrival.

■■

The pain that built me doesn't get to own me.

I'm writing my name on the rest of this story.

Becoming

I stopped chasing perfect.

Now I just want real.

■■

I used to flinch at the thought of changing.

Now I crave it.

Becoming

I kept growing, even when no one was clapping.

That's what becoming really is.

I don't need to be seen the way I used to.

I just want to see myself clearly.

Becoming

Some things didn't get closure.

They got distance.

And that's enough.

■■

Growth isn't loud.

Sometimes it's just not reacting the way you used
to.

Becoming

I didn't become fearless.

I just stopped letting fear answer first.

■■■

The world is spinning faster than I ever asked it
to.

But somehow, I've stopped trying to outrun it.

Becoming

I no longer need a witness to feel real.

That's how I know I've changed.

■■■

Even my silence feels different now.

It's not fear.

It's knowing I don't owe everyone an
explanation.

Forgiveness

I don't know if I forgive you.

But I don't want to carry it anymore.

That's a start.

■■■

I used to replay everything.

Now I just breathe through it.

Forgiveness

I forgive the version of you that didn't know better.

Even if the version you became never tried to.

■■

Some days, I forgive you entirely.

Other days, I forgive myself for not forgetting.

Forgiveness

It doesn't mean it didn't matter.

It means I've decided it won't become me.

■■

I don't want revenge

I want relief.

Forgiveness

I forgive the silence.

Even if it still stings.

■■

You thought I was overreacting.

I thought you'd understand.

We were both wrong, and I'm done punishing us
for it.

Forgiveness

I forgive the way you protected yourself.

Even when it meant losing me.

■■

I don't think she'll ever hear this.

So I'll forgive you for her.

Because someone has to.

Forgiveness

You hurt him more than he let on.

But he kept showing up anyway.

That counts as forgiveness.

And I'll honor it.

■■

Forgiveness isn't closure.

It's just making space for better things.

Forgiveness

I forgive the version of me that begged.

She just didn't want to be left alone.

■■■

I forgive you.

Not because you earned it.

But because I needed it.

Forgiveness

I'm still angry sometimes.

But I no longer mistake that for being stuck.

■■

You never said sorry.

But I stopped needing it to begin again.

Guilt

You needed honesty.

I gave you distance.

■ ■

There were so many chances to show up.

I kept waiting for a better version of me to take them.

Guilt

I was quiet when you needed backup.

You never said anything, but I still hear the silence.

You opened a door.

I stood in the hallway too long.

But I never stopped thinking about stepping in.

Guilt

You were the great friend.

I just didn't admit it until it was too late to notice.

■■■

I left without saying goodbye.

And called it self-preservation.

Maybe it was. But you still deserved more.

Guilt

I let the wrong version of me speak for too long.

I hate that.

■■■

I took you for granted.

Not because I didn't care.

But because you were always there.

And I assumed you always would be.

Guilt

Sometimes I feel guilty just for resting.

Like I'm breaking some rule I never agreed to.

I don't want to live by that kind of logic
anymore.

I wanted to be softer.

But I thought if I loved you less, it would hurt
less.

It didn't.

Guilt

I asked for honesty, then punished you for giving it.

I'm working on that.

■■

It wasn't just what I said.

It was the way I said it.

Like you were supposed to understand my damage without flinching.

Guilt

You always reached out first.

I didn't realize how much that meant until the messages stopped.

■■

You were patient.

I was unpredictable.

And I wish I'd seen that imbalance sooner.

Regret

I should've gotten off that train.

I still think about what might have started if I had.

■ ■

I should've asked what you meant.

Instead, I nodded and pretended I already knew.

Regret

You gave me a look like you were waiting for something.

I smiled.

I should've asked you to stay.

■■■

I kept it light because I was scared of what the truth would do.

Turns out silence did worse.

Regret

I regret how much I performed.

You were never asking for the polished version
of me.

■■ ■

We were standing right there.

I had the words.

And I still didn't say them.

Regret

I wish I'd taken the photo.

We looked happy.

And I didn't know it would be the last time.

■■

I thought I had more time to make it right.

Then suddenly someone shut off the light.

Regret

I waited for the perfect moment.

It never arrived.

So I departed.

■■

You deserved an explanation.

I showed you the exit instead

Regret

Sometimes I scroll back, looking for the message
I didn't send.

I still can't tell if it would've mattered.

But I wanted it to.

■ ■

There was a version of this story

Where on that train I turned around.

I still think about her.

Regret

I thought I had to prove I didn't care.

But I did.

So much.

■■

You were waiting for a reason to believe in me.

I regret how long I took to give you one.

Regret

I treated it like it was temporary.

Now I look back like it was everything.

■■

I regret how long I waited for permission

to want something different.

Jealousy

I wanted to be happy for you.

But part of me wondered why it wasn't me.

■■■■■■■■■■■■■■■■■■■■■■■■■■■■■■■■■■■■■

You told me your good news.

And I nodded.

Then went home and cried.

.

Jealousy

I know it wasn't a competition.

But I still felt like I lost.

■■

I saw your post and thought,

"Why do they get to be that free?"

Then I hated myself for thinking it.

Jealousy

You didn't replace me.

You just stopped needing me.

But somehow, that still hurt more.

■■

You got the job.

I showed the fake smile.

I wish I hadn't practiced it so much.

Jealousy

It wasn't just that you succeeded.

It was that you seemed so certain.

Like doubt never touched you the way it does
me.

■■■

I saw how easily you laughed with her.

I used to be your safe place.

Jealousy

You said "best friend" and it wasn't about me.

I didn't say anything, but something shifted after that.

∎∎∎∎∎∎∎∎∎∎∎∎∎∎∎∎∎∎∎∎∎∎∎∎∎∎∎∎∎∎∎∎∎∎∎∎∎ ∎∎

You don't know me.

But I've imagined living your life more than I want to admit.

Jealousy

I watched you step out of that car

like the world had never told you no.

I didn't even want the car. Just that kind of ease.

You described your dream person once.

And I spent months trying to fit it quietly.

Jealousy

I told myself I didn't care who you were seeing now.

But the truth is, I just hoped they were nothing like me.

■ ■

You loved her out loud.

I had to love you in silence.

That felt like a punishment.

Jealousy

I wasn't angry that you moved on.

I was angry that you didn't seem to look back.

■■

You looked at them the way I hoped you'd look at me. I smiled anyway.

That kind of pretending stayed with me

.

Anger

I did everything right.

And still ended up tired, anxious, and behind.

So tell me again how this system isn't broken.

■■■■■■■■■■■■■■■■■■■■■■■■■■■■■■■■■■■■■■

You knew exactly what you were doing.

That's the part I can't forgive.

Anger

I kept making excuses for you.

Until I realized you never asked me to.

Because you didn't care enough to notice.

You didn't misunderstand me.

You just preferred the version where you weren't the problem.

Anger

You didn't "accidentally" forget me.

You just chose not to carry me forward.

■■

You told your side like it was the only one.

And then acted surprised when I stopped
speaking.

Anger

You wanted the emotional intimacy of being loved, without the responsibility of being honest.

■■■

I didn't deserve your silence.

But I respected it more than your lies.

Anger

I wasn't difficult.

You were just too used to people saying yes.

■■■■■■■■■■■■■■■■■■■■■■■■■■■■■■■■■■■■■■■

You blamed me for reacting.

Never asked what caused it.

Anger

You loved how I made you feel.

Not who I actually was.

■■■

I used to think you were complicated.

Now I think you just liked control.

Anger

You played the victim in a story you wrote with your own head.

■ ■

This isn't bitterness.

It's clarity.

And it came later than I'd like — but not too late.

Anger

It taught us to measure our worth in output.

Then wondered why we burned out trying to be enough.

■■

It told us to be authentic.

Then punished us every time we were.

Loneliness

I sat in the group chat all day, but no one said my name.

■■■

Everyone talks.

But no one notices when I go quiet.

Loneliness

I'm not invisible.

I'm just not anyone's first thought.

■■

I used to reach out more.

Then I noticed how often I was the only one
doing it.

Loneliness

We all became our own tiny empires behind screens.

And then wondered why no one comes to visit.

■■

Everything is designed to keep us scrolling.

But nothing is built to hold us when its dark.

Loneliness

I know my neighbors' Wi-Fi names.

Not their voices.

■■■

We stopped fighting.

Now we just brush our teeth in silence.

Loneliness

I sleep beside you.

But I haven't felt held in months.

■■

You ask what's wrong.

But only when I'm already running on empty.

Too late for softness. Too tired to speak.

Loneliness

Even when I speak honestly,

I feel misunderstood in a language I was born into.

There are rooms inside me no one will ever visit.

And some days, that fact makes me feel unreachable.

Loneliness

I think I'm afraid there's no one coming.

Not in the metaphorical sense.

I mean really no one.

■ ■

You liked my insta story.

But didn't answer my message.

And somehow, that says everything.

Loneliness

I act connection all day.

But at night, I talk to a screen.

■■

Even loneliness has a Wi-Fi signal.

Moments

I stood under the trees and didn't check my phone.

That felt like something worth remembering.

■■■■■■■■■■■■■■■■■■■■■■■■■■■■■■■■■■■■■■■

We hugged like we both knew we'd never get it right again.

That was the first moment I wanted to stop time.

Moments

You laughed without looking at me.

I still think about the sound.

■■

That morning, the coffee was warm, the sun hit
the table, and no one needed anything from me.

Moments

I turned to tell you something,

and remembered you weren't there anymore.

■■

There was a second when you reached for my
hand but changed your mind.

I still hold it in my head.

Moments

You pulled your sleeves over your hands when
you got nervous.

I never said anything.

But I thought it was the most honest thing
anyone ever did

■■

The sunlight spilled across the kitchen floor.

I didn't take a photo.

I just stood in it.

Moments

The first time you said my name with softness.

I didn't show it, but I carried that moment
around all day.

■■

We didn't say goodbye.

But you looked back.

And that was something.

Moments

I remember the rain more than what we said.

It was the only thing that stayed gentle.

■■

You almost told me something.

Then blinked, smiled, and let it go.

I still wonder what it was.

Moments

Sometimes the moment doesn't need to be big.

It just needs to be real.

I heard a song in a café and forgot where I was.

For a few seconds, I was nineteen again.

Moments

You pressed my coat collar down before I walked out.

That was the moment I felt most seen.

■■

The sand shifted between my toes, and the waves said nothing back.

But I felt understood anyway.

Closure

You didn't say goodbye.

So I had to learn how to stop waiting.

■■■■■■■■■■■■■■■■■■■■■■■■■■■■■■■■■■■■■■■

We just stopped.

No conversation. No fire.

Just distance dressed as time.

Closure

You didn't leave dramatically.

You just became harder to reach.

■■

There were still things I wanted to say.

But none of them would've changed the silence
you gave me.

Closure

I replayed everything looking for a moment to fix.

Sometimes there isn't one.

■■

We didn't end badly. We just stopped needing each other in the same way.

And that's okay.

Closure

You ghosted me.

So I had to un-haunt myself.

■■

It wasn't closure I needed.

It was peace.

And I found it alone.

Closure

I don't hate you.

But I don't wish you well out loud anymore
either.

■■

It didn't end with a door slam.

It ended when I stopped hoping you'd knock.

Closure

You deleted the thread.

I memorized it.

■■■

There's no reply coming.

And somehow, that's not as sad as it used to be.

Closure

I still smile when I think of you.

That's how I know I've let it go.

■■■■■■■■■■■■■■■■■■■■■■■■■■■■■■■■■■■■■■

You were part of my story.

Not the whole thing.

And that's what makes it easier to turn the page.

Truths

It wasn't attention I wanted.

It was to feel chosen.

■■■ ■■

You didn't break my trust.

You just showed me where I'd placed it too quickly.

Truths

I wasn't overreacting.

I was reacting to being unheard for too long.

■■■ ■■

I made it look easy.

That's why no one asked if I was drowning.

Truths

I wanted to be enough.

But I also wanted to be seen.

■■■

It was never that I didn't care.

I just didn't think it was safe to show it.

Truths

We were taught to compete before we were taught to connect.

And now we wonder why we feel alone in a crowd.

■■■

They said we were free.

But everything we touched came with a price tag and a password.

Truths

I kept trying to explain myself.

Now I just pay attention to who listens the first time.

■■

The truth doesn't always fix things.

But it does let you stop pretending.

Truths

The truth is, I wasn't asking for much.

Just to be treated like I mattered.

■■

The truth is, life rarely gives closure.

It just hands you silence and expects you to grow around it.

Truths

The truth is, I shrank out of habit.

Not love.

■■■

The truth is, some people only know how to be
kind in the light.

They disappear when things get heavy.

Truths

The truth is, most people didn't really get me.

They just liked the parts that I posted with a filter on.

■■

The truth is, I thought healing would feel like progress.

It mostly just felt like patience.

Freedom

I stopped trying to make you proud.

And started making myself proud instead.

■ ■

You wanted a version of me you could explain.

I became a version I could live with.

Freedom

I am not my output.

And I don't need to collapse to earn rest.

■■

You don't get to measure our worth in what we produce.

We are done renting our souls to stay valid.

Freedom

You told me no one else would love me like you did.

You were right.

No one else hurt me and called it care.

■■■

You didn't break me.

You just taught me how badly I needed to walk away.

Freedom

I spent years shrinking my voice to feel safe.

Now I raise it for the ones who still can't.

■ ■

You asked me to "stay calm" in a world that doesn't.

But calm was never the problem.

Silence was.

Freedom

I used to open bills like they were threats.

Now I read them like paper. That's it. Just paper.

■■

Freedom didn't look like luxury.

It looked like breathing without math.

Freedom

I outgrew people I once begged to stay.

That's not ego. That's growth.

■■■■■■■■■■■■■■■■■■■■■■■■■■■■■■■■■■■■■■

She wasn't weak.

She just didn't know how many exits there really were.

Freedom

Your life looks perfect in pixels.

Mine feels real in silence.

I'll keep mine.

■■

I stopped chasing the timeline.

Some things bloom out of order and still become whole.

Freedom

I used to think keeping quiet made me easier to love.

Now I speak, and the right ones stay.

■■■■■■■■■■■■■■■■■■■■■■■■■■■■■■■■■■■■■■■

I don't need to be impressive.

I just need to feel like myself.

Freedom

They taught us endurance like it was a virtue.

But freedom is knowing when to walk away without apology.

■■

The weight of the world was never ours to carry alone.

They just hoped we wouldn't notice.

Freedom

We were never too much.

They just built the room too small.

■■■

They told us to be polished before we spoke.

We spoke anyway.

And that was freedom.

Thank you for reading *Unsent DMs*.

If something in these pages stayed with you, even for a moment; then I'm glad it found you.

For more of my writing, visit **farbellum.com**

And if you're looking for something with this same emotional resonance; quiet, honest, and made for people who feel deeply, I recommend *Notes for the Last Kind Ones*. It's a beautiful reflection by my colleague.

Remember you are never alone.

Estelle H.

www.ingramcontent.com/pod-product-compliance
Lightning Source LLC
Chambersburg PA
CBHW031625040426
42452CB00007B/686